72 Swimming Locations

LAKES ● RIVERS ● LIDOS

Wild Swimming RECORD BOOK

ADRIAN TIERNEY-JONES

First published 2010

The History Press
The Mill, Brimscombe Port
Stroud, Gloucestershire, GL5 2QG
www.thehistorypress.co.uk

British Library Cataloguing in Publication Data.
A catalogue record for this book is available from the British Library.

ISBN 978 0 7524 5713 0

Typesetting and origination by The History Press
Printed in Italy

Cover: © Getty Images
All other images from iStockphoto except: p.29 (courtesy of Henleaze Swimming Club); p.63 (courtesy of Adam Sparkes); p.71 (© Melanie Davies www.melaniedavies.co.uk); p.93 (Photograph by Klaus-Martin Hansche. This file is licensed under the Creative Commons Attribution-Share Alike 2.5 Generic license); p.121 © Alamy Images

CONTENTS

Introduction 6

Lakes of Mountain and Moorland 12
Magical Rivers 34
Relive the Golden Age of the Lido 58
Seaside Secrets 80
Pools, Ponds and Meres 104

Swimming Tips 124
Wild Swimming Safety 125
Water temperature 126
Waterlog 127
Waterworks 128

INTRODUCTION

I am on Exmoor, beneath the ramparts of the ancient hill fort of Cow Castle, a place of Iron Age antiquity that gleams with a summer coat of bright green bracken. High up here the River Barle cuts through the moorland. Beneath the west-facing shoulder of the hill, the river takes a right, deepens and provides an inviting pool on this hot summer's evening. It is an ideal place for a swim with only the sheep moving across the hillsides and the odd buzzard riding the overhead spirals of warm air for company.

The water is breathtakingly cold even though the sun has shone all through this July day. I gasp and contemplate coming out. My eleven-year-old son James scoffs and says that it's warm, but on the other hand he is wearing a wetsuit. Perseverance pays off, however, and I launch into the compact pool in the middle of the river. After the initial shock comes the rapture. The clear water is soft and lucid; it is also magnificently refreshing. What is most beguiling, reminiscent almost of the 'Piper at the Gates of Dawn' chapter in *The Wind in the Willows*, is the soothing sense of freedom and innocence that this swim evokes; a Proustian return to a childhood of simple pleasures. This is a different world from the treadmill of the roped-off lane in the municipal swimming pool. There is no sting of chlorine or string of proscribing notices. It is an activity free from the outside world, quiet and restful, calming and charming. This is the world of wild swimming, where rivers, lakes, ponds, coves and lidos are rediscovered and celebrated as an antidote to stress and modernity.

We did not know what we had lost until we found it again. Before the rise of the local swimming pool, wherever there was water Britons enjoyed it. Seaside towns were proud of their lidos, where swimming pageants and galas were the rock concerts of their day. Meanwhile, those with a penchant for quieter pleasures would seek out hidden coves and muddy estuaries. Young and old played and splashed in the shallows, while country kids could be glimpsed leaping off wooden platforms into slow-moving rivers; or they larked about and tired themselves out around reed-fringed meres and ponds. The rise of the concrete-and-chlorine local baths changed this, as municipal authorities and river boards decided that it was too risky to allow anyone to swim in their waters. Pollution also played its part.

However, our waters are cleaner and the tide has turned: more people are taking part in natural swimming. Wild swimming is the latest manifestation of our desire for a simpler and more honest life. It chimes with organic food, slow life and the search for the wilds, something a lot of us crave in this fast-moving, complex world. Within these pages are seventy-two places where you can swim wild and gain enlightenment through the medium of water, whether it's in a Scottish loch, a Welsh llyn, seaside lido or rural river.

Adrian Tierney-Jones

LAKES OF MOUNTAIN AND MOORLAND

You will find a goodly selection of lakes in which wild swimming comes into its own in the United Kingdom, whether it's a long loch, placid and peaceful amongst the heathery highlands of Scotland, or a Welsh llyn, all grey slate in colour, on a sunny day a mirror to the brooding, granite faced mountains of North Wales; and let's not forget the Cumbrian lakes of poetry and prose either. Many of these lakes are survivors from the Ice Age, left behind in deep hollows which the glaciers gorged out and then left when they melted away. They are cold and deep, some reputedly the haunts of imaginary creatures from a time of legends. Disregarding old tales, a swim in places like Loch Ness or Llyn Idwal is refreshingly icy, so be prepared for a dip that takes your breath away; others, such as Wast Water in Wasdale, at 79 metres the deepest lake in England, reach down into the earth, providing an extra thrill for the wild swimmer.

LLYN IDWAL

Nant Ffrancon, Snowdonia

Grid ref: SH 6459

Mountain swimming at its very best can be enjoyed in this deep blue-coloured glacial lake just off the A5, almost opposite the Ogwen Reservoir (where swimming is banned). A short hike up a path behind the youth hostel and warden centre will bring you into Cwm Idwal, where the lake sits at the centre of what feels like a three-sided amphitheatre, surrounded by tall crags and rock slabs, dotted by vast spreads of scree; the majestic peak of Tryfan is to your left. It's a popular swim, especially with climbers hoping to cool off after their exertions on the rocks. The water is deep and can get cold further out, so keeping close to the shore is always recommended. During the winter the surface can ice over; visit it then solely for sightseeing. Legend has it that a Welsh prince was drowned here and that for this reason no birds fly over the water.

Date: Weather: Your Rating: ☆ ☆ ☆ ☆ ☆

Notes:

HATCHMERE

Delamere Forest, Cheshire

Grid ref: SJ 553722

Hatchmere Lake can be found in Delamere Forest, Cheshire's largest area of woodland, and it's an easy place to find, being located on the main road north of Delamere railway station. During summer the temperature of the lake has been known to top a balmy 20°C, which no doubt has helped to make it a popular destination for serious wild swimmers and their families over many generations. Much of the attraction is in the sandy beach, warm shallows and grassy banks, where picnics and sun-bathing are the order of the day. Anglers also share the use of the lake, which in the 1990s caused some conflict and put the future of swimming in doubt. Fortunately an agreement was reached, partly through the efforts of local volunteers, who were inspired to set up the River and Lake Swimming Association. The Carriers Inn is directly opposite the lake and ideal for post-swim refreshments.

Date:

Weather:

Your Rating: ☆ ☆ ☆ ☆ ☆

Notes:

LOCH NESS

Drumnadrochit, Invernesshire, Highlands

Grid ref: NH 530288

If you want a Highland fling then a dip in the waters of Loch Ness might be just the job. Don't worry about the monster of legend (one recent theory held that Nessie was actually an erroneous sighting of circus elephants who were enjoying a splashabout in the 1930s). No one has ever been taken but it is wise not to be too complacent about the temperature of the water, which rarely gets above 10°C. This is nearly as cold as a pint of lager – so it goes without saying that wetsuits are highly recommended, as are beach shoes due to the rockiness of the foreshore. The Loch is dark in colour and becomes deep pretty quickly, so unless you are very experienced it's best to remain in the shallows close to the shoreline. Regulars to the loch often enter the water from a compact beach that stands opposite Urquhart Castle.

Date: Weather: Your Rating: ☆ ☆ ☆ ☆ ☆

Notes:

MELYNLLYN

Snowdonia

Grid ref: SH 7065

High up in the hills above the Conwy Valley, where the ravens croak and the sheep live their isolated lives, mountaineers and hikers can often be found taking a reviving dip in Melynllyn (translated as the Yellow Lake). Like many of its kindred watery spirits in Snowdonia, this isolated ice-cold, blue-grey lake was formed during the Ice Age and its shoreline is dotted with boulders left by the passing of the glaciers. Though partly surrounded by crags and cliffs to the west, there is more likelihood of a post-swim sunbathe here than there is by neighbouring Dulyn, which lies in shadow most of the day and has also been known to plunge to 55 feet within a few feet of the shore. This is a cooling and refreshing climax to a difficult but rewarding hike and on quiet (but warm!) days it might be conducive to a spot of discreet skinny-dipping!

Date: Weather: Your Rating: ☆ ☆ ☆ ☆ ☆

Notes:

5 CRUMMOCK WATER

Buttermere, Lake District, Cumbria

Grid ref: NY 175175

Even though there are plenty of heavenly swimming spots in the Lake District, Crummock Water is regarded as one of the most divine. For starters there's its position and views – the water's edge is fringed with woodland in many places, while the Grassmoor ridge stretches above it to the west. It's also a lot less popular than lakes such as Windermere. But there's another reason why this National Trust-owned lake is beloved of wild swimmers: water sports are banned on its surface, and the odd rowing boat is not so much of an irritant or danger. For swimmers who fancy a challenge and a spot of variety, Buttermere is just a short hike across green fields (the two of them might have been once joined), while the Lakes' highest waterfall – Scale Force – is very close by and ideal for a refreshing and rejuvenating shower beneath ice-cold water.

Date: Weather: Your Rating: ☆ ☆ ☆ ☆ ☆

Notes:

6 WAST WATER

Lake District, Cumbria

Grid ref: NY 176069

A classic Lake District plunge into crystal-clear and alpine-fresh water awaits in this magnificently remote Cumbrian lake, whose eastern shore rises up through a slope of broken scree to the majestic heights of Scafell Pike, the tallest mountain in England. Other peaks surrounding the lake include Red Pike, Kirk Fell and Great Gable. The lake is equally imposing, being 79 metres deep (no ancient legends of beasties with a penchant for swimmers' ankles here!) and 3 miles long. On a good day enjoy a swim into the centre of the lake through the mirrored reflections of the mountains and appreciate the views. This National Trust-owned lake is also boat-free, which adds to its allure. Rumour has it that somewhere in the depths there is a subterranean garden of gnomes complete with white picket fence, planted there in the past by some of the divers who appreciate the charms of Wast Water.

Date: Weather: Your Rating: ☆ ☆ ☆ ☆ ☆

Notes:

GORMIRE LAKE

Sutton Bank, Thirsk, North Yorkshire

Grid ref: SE 504833

Hidden away in the centre of the thick and mysterious Garbutt Wood is the semi-circular Gormire Lake, created during the Ice Age and home to several legends. One of them declares that the lake is bottomless and that there's a sunken village in the depths – another that a witch being chased once jumped into the lake and was taken by underwater currents to a well nine miles away (the lake is actually quite shallow). The sense of tranquillity that accompanies a dip in its cooling waters is amplified by the proximity of Sutton Bank, an escarpment that was much loved by the author James Herriot (we are, after all, in Herriot country). The lake is also popular with all manner of waterfowl, so you will find yourself sharing your dip with coot, great grebe and mallard. Approach it down a steepish track, off the Cleveland Way via the Sutton Bank Nature Trail.

Date:

Weather:

Your Rating: ☆ ☆ ☆ ☆ ☆

Notes:

HANMER MERE

Hanmer, Shropshire

Grid ref: SJ 454390

Hanmer is a small village on the Anglo-Welsh border and its mere forms part of a group of residual glacial lakes that are often collectively known as the Shropshire Lake District; it was a popular place for recreation during the First World War when troops were stationed in the area. In the summer, the water has been known to nudge 20°C, ideal for an enjoyable and warming dip; boats and fishermen are also rare. Frequent users recommend parking on the northern shore and then following a path through woodland to the eastern side where a sandy bay is ideal for entering the water. Good soft clean water is the reward, though because of debris on the bottom it is recommended that appropriate footwear be worn. Some wild swimmers have it that this is an ideal place for a spot of skinny-dipping – but this is very much up to the individual!

Date: Weather: Your Rating: ☆ ☆ ☆ ☆ ☆

Notes:

9 MALHAM TARN

Nr Settle, North Yorkshire

Grid ref: SD 895663

Malham Tarn is one of the highest lakes in England and acted as the inspiration for Charles Kingsley's Victorian tear-jerker *The Water Babies*. Being in the Yorkshire Dales and not that far from Settle, Malham is at the heart of good walking country, so on a hot day a dip in this ancient glacial lake is excellent for cooling down. It's not a deep lake and it is also a wetland nature reserve; you will be sharing the water with various wildfowl such as curlew and mallards, so make sure you don't disturb them. Also note that you can only get into the water from the east side. On the other hand, if you fancy a reviving natural shower then nearby is Janet's Foss, a waterfall and deep pool that was once used for washing sheep after they had been sheared. This is also an ideal place for a picnic.

Date: Weather: Your Rating: ☆ ☆ ☆ ☆ ☆

Notes:

LOCH LOMOND

10 Nr Inversnaid, Stirlingshire

Grid ref: NN 332100

Situated in the Loch Lomond and Trossachs National Park, this world-famous loch is one of the largest freshwater lakes in the United Kingdom, which makes it an invigorating (600 feet to the bottom at its deepest point means that it is cold) challenge to long-distance swimmers. If the thought of spending at least fifteen hours immersed in the Loch for the sake of covering almost the same distance as if you were crossing the English Channel doesn't appeal, wild swimmers can choose a less demanding dip to be found on the northern side, close to Rob Roy's cave (this is signposted off the Highland Way, which you can join from Inversnaid). Here the water is entered by scrambling down a rocky and wooded slope just below the cave. The Rob Roy theme continues to the north at the top of the Loch where his 'bathtub' can be found – a plunge pool beneath the invigorating Fallach Falls.

Date: Weather: Your Rating: ☆ ☆ ☆ ☆ ☆

Notes:

LLYN CAU

11 Cadair Idris, Snowdonia

Grid ref: SH 718124

It has long been said that those who spend a night on the summit of Cadair Idris (translated as the Chair of Idris) will either become insane or go on to fame and fortune as a great poet. This mountain seems to attract myths, as it was also supposed to be the hunting grounds of the Welsh hounds of hell. Llyn Cau, a beautiful glacial lake that lingers 400 metres below in the shadow of Cadair Idris, also has its stories: it is supposed to be bottomless and home to the *afanc*, a Welsh version of the Loch Ness Monster that has a penchant for snacking on those who enter its domain. However, monsters are the last thing on the mind of those who bathe in its cool and refreshing depths and just enjoy the experience. It's a bit of a hike to get to this llyn, which means that if you are heading for it on a hot summer's day then you will be glad of a cooling dip by the time you arrive.

Date: Weather: Your Rating: ☆ ☆ ☆ ☆ ☆

Notes:

12 HENLEAZE LAKE

Westbury-on-Trym, Bristol

Grid ref: ST 581775

This is a former quarry fed by spring water, and is only 3 miles from the centre of Bristol. Established in 1919, the club has access to 100 metres of water, which varies in depth from 3 metres to 6 beneath the diving area. Various varieties of trees and green lawns surround the lake, an environment that makes for a tranquil swim in what feels more like some rural arcadia than the edge of one of England's busiest cities (suburban housing estates surround the lake within its wooded hideaway). Those with a penchant for high diving will make for the four platforms. The only downside is that, as the lake is run by Henleaze Swimming Club, it is accessible only to members – and there's a three-year waiting list. However, swimmers have been known to badger their way in as members are allowed two guests. The lake is shared with anglers.

Date: Weather: Your Rating: ☆ ☆ ☆ ☆ ☆

Notes:

13 LLYN TEGID

Llanuwchllyn, Gwynedd

Grid ref: SH 900330

Disregarding man-made reservoirs, Llyn Tegid (or Bala Lake) is the largest lake in Wales, sited just south of the Welsh-speaking town of Bala – its considerable size has made it a Mecca for triathletes. Watersports are also popular, while anglers are drawn to the shores due to the abundance of fish, so wild swimmers should always take care. The B4403 runs along the southern side of the lake (parallel to the small steam engine line) providing ample places for parking and entering the water. For those who like to boast of swimming with monsters, a dip in the cold waters makes an interesting Welsh counterpart to Loch Ness; like the famous loch, it is also reputedly the home of a water monster, affectionally known as Teggie. The other myth that is attached to the lake is that it is home to the palace of King Tegid, and that ethereal buildings are occasionally seen on moonlit nights.

Date: Weather: Your Rating: ☆ ☆ ☆ ☆ ☆

Notes:

14 LAKE WINDERMERE

Windermere, Cumbria

Grid ref: SD 393981

Although the largest freshwater lake in England is better known for the fleet of pleasure boats that criss-cross its surface, could it give Loch Ness a run for its monster-sighting money? Some think so, especially as one cameraman filmed an unexplained series of ripples on the water in 2009 (in fact, reports of something odd in the water stretch back to the 1950s and the creature has been christened Bownessie). However, wild swimmers are a hardy bunch and not to be deterred, with speedboats more of a concern than anything that could call Nessie a close cousin. There are two recommended spots where Windermere can be entered – Millerground Landing and Red Nab, both of which are very close to the town of Windermere. Those who have enjoyed a dip there usually suggest turning up in the early morning so as to avoid the crowds, and keeping close to the shore is always recommended.

Date: Weather: Your Rating: ☆ ☆ ☆ ☆ ☆

Notes:

MAGICAL RIVERS

Splashing about in the river was a commonplace activity for country kids before the coming of the municipal swimming pool with its mantle of concrete and bouquet of chlorine. Summer afternoons, straight after school, off they would go to spend many a contented hour ducking and diving in their local river, most having learnt to swim in these same contented waters. Now this innocent and childlike pleasure is rediscovered as our rivers are once again clean and unpolluted. The joy of a river comes from the soft and soothing feel of the water as you pass through it, as well as the sense of closeness to nature. There are also the changing moods of a river. Some are slow and sluggish, encouraging the wild swimmer to float and linger, to become as one with the water; others boast deep pools or brisk waterfalls that set the skin glowing and give the senses a wake-up call.

THE WYE

Parc Waun Capel, Rhayader

Grid ref: SO 967683

The Wye is the great river of South Wales, even if it does meet its destiny in England. There are plenty of stretches where swimming can be enjoyed though it is not a river to be treated lightly – if it has been pouring with rain high up in the hills, then what might have been a slow-moving and graceful body of water can become torrential quite quickly. In the bustling market town of Rhayader there is a shingle beach below the town bridge, though it is recommended that swimmers keep away from a pool that sits directly upstream of the same bridge, where the current is strong. However, there is good swimming to be had at several spots further up at Waun Capel Park; below the metal footbridge the water runs down a cascade which provides a lively wake-up call on a sluggish morning. Another spot on the Wye where swimmers congregate is the Warren at Hay-on-Wye (SO 222425).

Date: Weather: Your Rating: ☆ ☆ ☆ ☆ ☆

Notes:

THE THAMES

Lechlade, Gloucestershire

Grid ref: SU 205989

It is said that the Thames at the small market town of Lechlade is the furthest up the river that large craft, such as narrowboats, can navigate. Proof of this is manifest in Lechlade's famous Ha'Penny Bridge, so named because it was supposed to be the toll for boats starting off downriver. The bridge has another use: it has long been used for local children as a jumping-off point for the river below (there is an equally long tradition of it being popular for diving competitions). Swimming down the Thames is also popular out here – many start on the southern side off the Riverside Park and enjoy the prospect of drifting down one of the most famous rivers in the world. There is also a pleasing pool where the small tributary of the Coln joins the Thames. More wild swimming can be found at the nearby Buscott Lock.

Date: Weather: Your Rating: ☆ ☆ ☆ ☆ ☆

Notes:

3 THE CAM

Grantchester Meadows, Grantchester, Cambridge Grid ref: TL 445571

This is the famous stretch of river that Rupert Brooke and his fellow aesthetes claimed as their own during the years leading up to the First World War. A century on, to take a dip in the slow-moving Cam off these lush and luxuriant water meadows is to experience some of the sensuality and sheer pleasure of that doomed generation: willows dangle over the slow-moving river, while punts and the odd canoe glide languidly by. Meanwhile, moorhens briefly disturb the water as they dart across the river. The Cam here is clear and clean, though the bottom can be muddy. It might be a cliché but on the right day, this is a magical swim. After the last house on Grantchester Road there is a path that goes down to the river; from here you can take your pick of spots. After your swim wander into the village and relax at the Orchard Tea Garden.

Date: Weather: Your Rating: ☆ ☆ ☆ ☆ ☆

Notes:

4 THE PLYM

Cadover Bridge, Devon, nr Shaugh Prior

Grid ref: SX 554646

The Plym tumbles down from Dartmoor, and upstream from where it passes beneath Cadover Bridge there is a plethora of pools and waterfalls that offer the chance for a bracing plunge or shower. Some of the pools are compact and only suitable for one person, while others offer enough space for a family splash. The water is clean and bracing, though it is stained by peat (this is harmless). It's a scenic place: not only are you taking a dip amid the splendour of Dartmoor, but some stretches of the river are dotted with grassy islands that are bound to encourage a sense of adventure in many children. This is a popular place with local wild swimmers, but such is the abundance of pools that no-one should ever find themselves lacking space for a swim. If the weather is sunny, there are also plenty of sunbathing spots.

Date: Weather: Your Rating: ☆ ☆ ☆ ☆ ☆

Notes:

5 THE USK

Crickhowell Bridge, Powys

Grid ref: SO 215181

Crickhowell is a lively little town that has grown up on the northern bank of the Usk, a river that rises in the Carmarthen Fans Mountains. Sitting between the Black Mountains and the Brecon Beacons the town is much visited by those with a love of outdoor pursuits. Down by the Usk you will find a medieval bridge that, uniquely, has sixteen arches on one side and seventeen on the other – the water runs from deep to shallow downstream. However, upstream from here, alongside Bulpit Meadows, those in the know have long enjoyed a dip in Galvey Pool, where many years ago a local man would teach the town's children to swim (some say by throwing them into the water!). It was also here that a swimming gymkhana would be held annually. The Usk has several spots where swimming can be enjoyed, including some near where it passes through Brecon.

Date: Weather: Your Rating: ☆ ☆ ☆ ☆ ☆

Notes:

THE BARLE

6

Cow Castle, Simonsbath, Somerset

Grid ref: SS 793375

Along with the Exe and the Lyn, the Barle is one of Exmoor's major rivers. It rises amid the Chains, an isolated and wild part of northern Exmoor noted for its harsh terrain. It eventually joins with the Exe just below the town of Dulverton. Its gin-clear waters offer many opportunities for wild swimming, especially after it has travelled past the small village of Simonsbath (traditionally known as the capital of Exmoor). As well as a popular spot near Landacre Bridge a couple of miles west of Withypool, a less crowded stretch for a swim can be found at a bend in the river as it flows beneath the Iron Age ramparts of Cow Castle (supposedly built by fairies). Follow the path alongside the Barle out of Simonsbath and you will get to Cow Castle within 2 miles. Take a dip here to cool off as you take a perambulation through this beautiful countryside.

Date: Weather: Your Rating: ☆ ☆ ☆ ☆ ☆

Notes:

7 THE THAMES

Clifton Hampden, Oxfordshire

Grid ref: SU 549955

As well as providing many opportunities for wild swimming, the Thames has long been a source of literary inspiration. Mole and Ratty lived the life aquatic in *The Wind in the Willows*, while Jerome K. Jerome's trio of cheery chaps took to the water in a boat and mused on life. Jerome obviously took his research for *Three Men in a Boat* seriously; he was very taken with this delightful part of the Lower Thames, and no wonder. The village of Clifton Hampden has an eminently tranquil spot for a swim through a bucolic and soothing landscape of wild meadows (though it is important that swimmers watch out for boats). Enter the water next to the village bridge (the Barley Mow, a thatched pub much praised by Jerome is close by) where you will find sandy bays that slope gently into deeper water towards the other side of the river.

Date: Weather: Your Rating: ☆ ☆ ☆ ☆ ☆

Notes:

THE THAMES

Port Meadow, Oxford

Grid ref: SP 4908

This gently curving stretch of the Thames is a short walk from the railway station, just north of the Oxford suburb of Jericho. It's an area that is said to have inspired Lewis Carroll when he came to write *Alice in Wonderland*. At 440 acres, Port Meadow is the largest part of common land in the city and there are plenty of places from which to enter the water. Some suggest crossing the footbridge at the southern end of the meadow and entering the water at the Binsey side. Staying on the eastern side though there are several little beaches that are very popular with families and a dip in the cool Thames in the company of various wildfowl is heavenly. Another option is to walk upriver to Wolvercote and swim in the Thames there – afterwards a further literary connection can be enjoyed with a drink at the Trout Inn, which was a favourite of Inspector Morse.

Date: Weather: Your Rating: ☆ ☆ ☆ ☆ ☆

Notes:

9 THE TEME

Ludlow, Shropshire

Grid ref: SO511752

Ludlow is one of the finest market towns in England and is well noted for its excellent food shops. However, what is not so celebrated is that the River Teme, which curls its way through the town, has a well-liked spot used by swimmers for generations (there's even a notice in the vicinity that celebrates the history and tradition of wild swimming in the Teme). Those in the know suggest entering the water off an old jetty in the Linney Riverside Park, which sits in the shadow of Ludlow's magnificently distressed castle. This is definitely a spot for a relaxing dip, with the water running pretty slowly, though it is deep and the presence of a nearby weir downstream means that you should be fairly confident of your swimming abilities. A car park is close by, though Ludlow is such a lovely place that it would be a shame not to wander through its streets.

Date: Weather: Your Rating: ☆ ☆ ☆ ☆ ☆

Notes:

THE OUSE

Barcombe Mills, nr Lewes

Grid ref: TQ435148

You will find Barcombe Mills several miles north of Lewes. This grassy stretch of riverside space is popular with families in the summer, who either drop into the water or just sit back and relax on the grassy banks. As the Ouse makes its grand and stately way downstream there are several places where a splash and a swim in its cooling waters have long been a local favourite (you might even see members of the Brighton Swimming Team practicing their 'survival swimming' fully-clothed if the sea is rough!). The water is clean and very slow-moving so this is definitely one for moderate swimmers. This popular stretch can be found by leaving your vehicle at a car park close to Barcombe House and then walking along a path upstream. This is a wide stretch of river and on cool summer days it can take some time to warm up.

Date: Weather: Your Rating: ☆ ☆ ☆ ☆ ☆

Notes:

THE ERME

Ivybridge, Devon

Grid ref: SX 637571

Ivybridge sits on the southern edge of Dartmoor and through it rushes the Erme, coming down off the moor in an urgent cascade of water, leaping over stones and swirling around rocks, vanishing behind bridges as it passes through the town. On first glance the idea of a wild swim doesn't look too promising, but those in the know head for a parking spot underneath the railway viaduct. From there it's suggested that all wild swimmers follow the river upstream through Long Timber Woods, and after approximately 40 metres a series of pools will be encountered. The first is the Lovers' Pool, appropriately dark and shaded beneath the trees, then a further stroll will lead to the Higher Weir Pool. Looking for an even quieter swim? Carry on upwards and there is Trainman's Pool. The river is popular with kayaks and canoes so keep an eye out for them.

Date: Weather: Your Rating: ☆ ☆ ☆ ☆ ☆

Notes:

12 THE WHARFE

Bolton Abbey, nr Skipton, North Yorkshire

Grid ref: SE 076543

The Wharfe rises in the Yorkshire Dales and one of the places it passes on its way to join the Ouse is Bolton Abbey, a striking-looking set of ecclesiastical ruins. Alongside the banks of the river there is a winsome stretch of beach, a mix of sand and pebble, that is very popular with families – this is a spot where youngsters can paddle and splash themselves in perfect safety (the Wharfe has a reputation for rising to spate very quickly). The surroundings of green parkland and trees also give the place an extra sense of beauty. For those who want to have more of a swim there are deeper spots slightly upstream. As you can imagine a hot sunny day will see the crowds out so this is not a place for a quiet and reflective dip. The abbey was a victim of the Dissolution of the Monasteries in 1539 – could the monks ever have imagined that their haven would become so popular?

Date:　　Weather:　　Your Rating: ☆ ☆ ☆ ☆ ☆

Notes:

THE WAVENEY

13 Outney Common, Bungay, Suffolk

Grid ref: TM 334908

The Waveney is the river most associated with Roger Deakin, a river in which he memorably once wrote about how he had disturbed an otter whilst taking a swim in the same waters as this magical and seldom-seen creature. Deakin was bewitched by the encounter. Living out in Suffolk not far from its banks, he saw the Waveney as his home river and never tired of its many charms. Many others feel the same, as it is slow-moving and gentle, taking the swimmer through a landscape of gorgeous water-meadows, woodland and marshes before it hits the sea. It's a river that is meant to be swum and many of its devotees suggest joining it as it curves around Outney Common, a watery bulb-shaped piece of land to the north-west of Bungay. It's a charming river, a comfortable and safe channel, though it is suggested that you should always keep an eye open for canoeists.

Date: Weather: Your Rating: ☆ ☆ ☆ ☆ ☆

Notes:

THE HELFORD

Helford Passage, Cornwall

Grid ref: SW 765265

Roger Deakin once swam across this stately and well-mannered Cornish river at low tide and found himself immersed in the estuary mud and slime before he reached deeper water. However, if you start your swim at a higher tide then it's clear water all the way, including a span where salt and fresh water commingle and commune, taking the swimmer through cold and warmer currents almost as if he were in some sort of treatment bath. The Helford Passage is on the northern side of the river and whilst doing the swim it is recommended that colourful bathing hats be worn so that boaters know that there are people in the water; if possible, get a friend along with an inflatable for extra protection. Also be aware of the pedestrian ferry. This is a delightful swim and afterwards swimmers can relax in Helford's pub before taking a short trip to the romantic Frenchman's Creek of Daphne Du Maurier fame.

Date: Weather: Your Rating: ☆ ☆ ☆ ☆ ☆

Notes:

THE CONWY

15 Fairy Glen, Betws-y-Coed

Grid ref: SH 801543

The fairy folk might have given their name to this gorge through which the Conwy travels on its way to greet the sea at the town of the same name. There's certainly a sense of romance in taking a swim through its steep sided environs, but the old Welsh name was much more commonplace: Ffôs Noddyn, or the Ditch of the Chasm. It is a rugged place to which you descend by a path after paying a small entrance fee (for the upkeep of the access). Several large rocks are dotted about the rivers, places of rest on which swimmers often sit, and there's a fairly deep section in the middle of the gorge. Wooded banks and rock walls clothed with vegetation also add to the attraction. It's situated just outside the town of Betws-y-Coed which in the summer is crowded – the glen provides a peaceful haven, especially if visited in the early morning.

Date: Weather:  Your Rating:  ☆ ☆ ☆ ☆ ☆

Notes:

RELIVE THE GOLDEN AGE OF THE LIDO

If you think that taking the plunge in an outdoor lido has something in common with visiting your local indoor pool, then think again. The lido, which had its heyday in the years between the world wars, is outside and at the mercy of the mercurial British climate, so the water is much colder (there's always the prospect of a warm shower afterwards though). On the plus side there's no chlorine. Some, such as the Jubilee Pool in Penzance, hark back to the golden age, while others are much younger and lack the art deco finesse of their more venerable cousins. Outdoor pools, as opposed to stately lidos, are situated right next to the sea and are washed and filled with each tide (you might even find the odd fish swimming about!) These are especially suitable for young swimmers who might struggle with unexpected waves or tidal currents. There are over 100 lidos and outdoor pools in the UK, so there's no excuse for not searching out the nearest one to you.

TOPSHAM SWIMMING POOL

1

Fore Street, Topsham, Devon

Tel: 01392 874477

Compared to the more venerable open air pools that have seen decades of enjoyment, Topsham's compact but cosy pool only came into being in the late 1970s – mainly as a result of the hard work of a few individuals who galvanised the community to support its construction. This heated outdoor pool is better for those of a less robust constitution than, say, the swimmer who reveals in the chill and cold of somewhere like Penzance's Jubilee Pool (though there is a dedicated and hardy bunch of locals who use the pool from 6–8.30 am every day). It is 25 metres in length and varies in depth from 1 to 3 metres. And, as if to underline its appeal to the swimmer with a penchant for taking a few lengths in comparative warmish luxury, roof-mounted solar panels help to keep water temperatures at a constant 80–83˚F. Open May–September.

Date: Weather: Your Rating: ☆ ☆ ☆ ☆ ☆

Notes:

2 ILKLEY LIDO

Denton Road, Ilkley, West Yorkshire

Tel: 01943 600453

A pleasing example of art deco (it received Grade II Listed status in 2009) that was constructed to honour George V's jubilee in 1935. This lido lies in the shadow of the famous Ilkley Moors and has long been popular with those who seek escape through the medium of water rather than moorland. It can only be described as lagoon-shaped and it offers easy swimming, which makes it popular with families. There is a slide (sadly the diving board and baby chute fell foul of health and safety regulations) and an outdoor fountain. Once you've taken a dip, there are plenty of places around the pond to enjoy a picnic and there is also a café that sells bacon sarnies and the like. Open May–September, but there is a heated indoor pool alongside for those who cannot leave the water alone in the winter.

Date: Weather: Your Rating: ☆ ☆ ☆ ☆ ☆

Notes:

3

TINSIDE LIDO

Hoe Road, Plymouth, Devon

Tel: 01752 261915

Situated off Plymouth Hoe this is another wonderful example of art deco design, a much-loved Plymouth institution that opened in 1935 and became noted for its beauty competitions and elegance (swimmers were sometimes serenaded by poolside orchestras). As with so many lidos, the post-war years saw Tinside fall into decline as local people headed off abroad for warmer climes and sunnier beaches – it suffered from neglect and was closed in 1992. However, the swimmers of Plymouth were not to be deterred; a determined campaign saved the lido and it reopened in 2003. It also gained Grade II listed status and substantial investment has brought it back to its former glory. It uses treated sea water and has a fine fountain in the middle. If this is not enough, there are several tidal pools that have been built into the nearby rocks, alongside high diving boards. Opens May–September.

Date: Weather: Your Rating: ☆ ☆ ☆ ☆ ☆

Notes:

OPEN

4 CAMBRIDGE JESUS GREEN POOL

Chesterton Road, Cambridge

Tel: 01223 302579

Academic types who yearn for an open-air dip could do worse than taking themselves off to this lengthy yet slimline pool. At 90 metres it is one of the largest of its kind in Europe and was built and opened with great ceremony in 1923. Located next to the south side of the River Cam (within earshot of the traffic that passes by just across the river) it is a natural haven for both the outdoor swimmer who craves the adrenalin high of cold water and those who like to soak up the sun. Another striking and comfortable feature is the surrounding screen of tall and long-established trees that help to act as a natural windbreak. Curiously enough, the pool's deepest part (2.5 metres) is said to be in the middle, which means that families can splash about in the shallows at both ends. Opens May–September.

Date: Weather: Your Rating: ☆ ☆ ☆ ☆ ☆

Notes:

CIRCENCESTER OPEN AIR SWIMMING POOL

Riverside Walk, Thomas Street, Cirencester Tel: 01285 653947

Queen Victoria was just over halfway through her reign when a group of local businessmen decided that the citizens of Circencester would benefit from an outdoor swimming pool. The enterprise opened in 1870, thus making it one of the oldest of its kind in the country, though it was only through the efforts of local volunteers in the 1970s that it was kept open. It's not the largest of pools, being 27 metres long and 1.8 metres at its deepest, but it has a charm all of its own. It is also still supplied by water pumped from a nearby spring, as it was when first opened, although this is now heated. There is a large paddling pool for youngsters (older children can have a go at water polo sessions in the summer) and there is a simple 'tuck shop' where a hot drink might be just the job after a dip. It can be found close to Cirencester Park and opens May–September.

Date: Weather: Your Rating: ☆ ☆ ☆ ☆ ☆

Notes:

6 DANCING LEDGE

Langton Matravers, nr Swanage, Dorset

Grid ref: SY 997768

Wild swimming in the shadow of the Jurassic Coast can be enjoyed with style at Dancing Ledge, a salt-water pool that was cut (some say blasted) out of the base of a cliff that once did time as a quarry for Purbeck stone; it got its name because it is the size of a ballroom floor. A far cry from the elegant and stylish surrounds of a classic lido, this honest and earthy pool was created with the pupils of a local prep school in mind back in the early years of the twentieth century. John Betjeman mentioned it in his poem 'Hearts Together'. The surrounding area is popular with rock climbers and the descent down the slope to the pool involves a small bit of scrambling which could daunt some, though swimming in the clear and cold water as the tide creeps up the shore is ample reward.

Date: Weather: Your Rating: ☆ ☆ ☆ ☆ ☆

Notes:

STONEHAVEN OPEN AIR SWIMMING POOL

Queen Elizabeth Park, Stonehaven, Aberdeenshire Tel: 01569 762134

Stonehaven is a former fishing port a few miles south of Aberdeen; with the Highlands behind and the North Sea in front you would have thought that outdoor swimming here would be as likely as a kilt on a cockney. However, they are a tough lot up here as the popularity of their magnificent open-air art deco Olympic-size pool shows. Situated at the northern end of the town's long sandy beach, this heated and fully-filtrated salt water pool celebrated its seventy-fifth anniversary in 2009, though like many other lidos of its kind it went through hard times in the 1990s when it nearly closed. It was only due to the efforts of dedicated locals that it was saved. With brightly-painted terraces for viewing, a slide and a newly opened paddling pool, it's very popular with families, while serious swimmers take advantage of the legendary midnight swims. Opens May–September.

Date: Weather: Your Rating: ☆ ☆ ☆ ☆ ☆

Notes:

8 NANTWICH OUTDOOR BRINE POOL

Wall Lane, Nantwich, Cheshire

Tel: 01270 537255

Enjoy a warm and salty swim in what is thought to have been the last remaining brine pool in the UK until Droitwich Lido Spa re-opened in 2007. Built in 1934 and opened to the public that same year, Nantwich's unique pool gets its brine pumped up from an underground source; the saline-rich water helps to keep the pool clean and thankfully there is no need for chlorine as a result. Those with a yen for Mediterranean-style bathing will love the fact that the temperature is kept at 74°C and becomes even warmer on one of those rare days when the sun shines and the mercury climbs. It's popular with both local families and visitors to Nantwich. There's no pleasing everyone though – some of the older regulars have been known to grumble that the pool is not as cold as it was when they were youngsters splashing about in the shallows. Opens May–September.

Date: Weather: Your Rating: ☆ ☆ ☆ ☆ ☆

Notes:

9 SALTDEAN LIDO

Saltdean, Brighton

Tel: 01273 880616

If the years between the wars saw the golden age of the lido they also saw the construction of many new towns on what had previously been farmland. Saltdean was one such town and naturally it had a lido. It opened towards the end of the 1930s and was acclaimed for its stylish design – it is overlooked on one side by a curved building that looks not unlike the bridge of an ocean liner. Like many other lidos in the postwar era decline set in and it looked as if it would be closed for good, but it was reopened in 1998 by the then sports minister Tony Banks. It is separated from the sea by the main coast road that links Brighton and Newhaven, so a swim in the compact pool can often be accompanied by the roar of passing traffic. With a children's pool as an added attraction, this is a really family-friendly place. Call to check opening times. At the time of writing the Lido is under threat of redevelopment.

Date: Weather: Your Rating: ☆ ☆ ☆ ☆ ☆

Notes:

SALTDEAN LIDO

10 PELLS OUTDOOR SWIMMING POOL

Brook Street, Lewes, East Sussex

Tel: 01273 472334

There's been swimming on this site since the 1860s when a brick-lined pool was built. This makes Pells the oldest fresh-water swimming pool in the country, and over 150 years after the first slab of turf was dug Lewes folk still enjoy a dip in its spring-water-fed confines. In common with most other outdoor pools, Pells has had a brush with mortality: it was nearly closed and turned into a skateboard park in the 1990s but over 4,000 local people signed a petition to keep it open. It's not big – 40 metres by 20 metres – but many swear by a relaxing swim in its soft, soothing waters, while there is also a leafy sunbathing area and a paddling pool for youngsters. Open May–September; please note that if you're heading out for a swim in rainy weather it's best to contact the pool as it often closes early during inclement conditions.

Date: Weather: Your Rating: ☆ ☆ ☆ ☆ ☆

Notes:

11 BUDE SEA POOL

Summerleaze Beach, Bude, Cornwall

Tel: 01208 262822

Sometimes swimmers find themselves sharing the water with fish or even the odd surfer washed over the wall of this much-loved outdoor pool that was carved from slate rock in the 1930s. The local Thynne family put up half the money for its construction, an act for which swimmers have been thanking them ever since. You will also find fronds of seaweed floating about while shifting sands cover the bottom of the pool; since depth can vary, diving is a no-no. The pool found itself under threat of closure several years ago due to concerns over health and safety, but thankfully it has survived and offers a safer alternative to salt-water swimmers than the sea off Bude, which can have its moments of treachery. This is a gorgeous spot for a swim, sitting as it does at the base of a cliff – while sunbathing with a view over the Atlantic as the rollers come in also has its attractions. Open May–September.

Date: Weather: Your Rating: ☆ ☆ ☆ ☆ ☆

Notes:

12 JUBILEE POOL

The Promenade, Penzance, Cornwall

Tel: 01736 369224

The Jubilee Pool was constructed during the golden age of outdoor lidos, opening in 1935, George V's jubilee year. It was built on the site of a popular Penzance bathing spot – the Battery Rocks – triangular in shape and surrounded by streamlined walls so that it could withstand the battering of the sea when conditions become rough. Terraces were also constructed for spectators and sunbathers. Like many an inter-war lido it fell on hard times and by the start of the 1990s closure looked on the cards. However, the Jubilee Pool Association was formed and campaigned to bring this great Penzance institution back to life. By 1994, it had been renovated and was re-opened. It is now a graceful and elegant pool that also has an area where youngsters can paddle and splash to their heart's content. This art deco delight is the largest outdoor seawater swimming pool in the UK. Open May–September.

Date: Weather:  Your Rating: ☆ ☆ ☆ ☆ ☆

Notes:

13 TOOTING BEC LIDO

Tooting Bec Road, London SW16 1RU Tel: 0208 871 7198

Outdoor swimming in the inner city is never cooler than when it's at Tooting Bec Lido, one of the largest freshwater pools in England and a favourite with swimmers from across south London. It opened in 1906 when men and women had to swim at separate times (mixed bathing finally came in 1931) and was originally called the Tooting Bathing Lake, only becoming known as a lido during the 1930s. In the 1990s it was on the verge of closure, until the South London Swimming Club (the oldest swimming club in the UK call the lido their 'home pool') stepped in to manage matters. Even though the lido is slap-bang in the urban conurbation of south London, a tranquil sense of peace and quiet accompanies a morning dip in the clear, cold and fresh waters, thanks to the muffling effect of the trees that surround the place.

Date: Weather: Your Rating: ☆ ☆ ☆ ☆ ☆

Notes:

THE POOL

Portreath, nr Redruth

A natural rock pool can be found on the east side of Portreath's sandy beach close to the harbour wall. This tidal swimming pool is just one of the joys of this small north Cornish village whose nearest town is Redruth; surfers and windsurfers also enjoy themselves in the waters of the cove. One side of the pool was blocked in at some stage in the past, thus forming the swimming pool, and when the tide is out or the seas are rough it makes for a safe and refreshing place, especially for youngsters. Up until the 1970s it was used as a natural swimming pool for local schoolchildren. On the other side of the beach there are also six baths that were cut into the rock in the nineteenth century – they are known as Lady Basset's Baths. Her father was a great believer in the recuperative powers of sea water.

Date: Weather: Your Rating: ☆ ☆ ☆ ☆ ☆

Notes:

SEASIDE SECRETS

If you like to be beside the seaside but also like to remain far from the madding crowd then a hidden cove, isolated beach or secret bay is an ideal place for a spot of wild swimming. Sandy beaches recall the joy of childhood holidays as you run into the waves and let the bracing seawater bring you to life – if you've got children with you then don't forget to rock pool! Or will it be a secluded bay studded with rocks that can provide diving platforms, with the gulls wheeling and crying overhead? How about a lonely cove, where the only sound will be the clatter and chatter of shingle as the waters drag and dredge the pebbles with each wave? Places like Angel's Bay on the North Wales coast or the long stretch of sand off the Suffolk village of Walberswick offer plenty of opportunities for the wild swimmer to dip their toes in the water and enjoy.

WALBERSWICK BEACH

Walberswick, Suffolk

Grid ref: TM 496743

Walberswick is so pretty it hurts: roses round the door, pristine village green, annual crabbing contest, two excellent pubs serving Adnams' famous ales and, for the wild swimmer, waves gently slapping against the sandy, shingle-backed, gently sloping beach. The water is bracing and ideal for one of those early morning swims that clear away the cobwebs of the night before. Be aware that once in the water the beach shelves quite steeply into deep water, so caution is needed when the waves get lively. It's a long softly-curving beach that, if walked, will take you all the way to the legendary lost town of Dunwich, now crumbling ruins receding into the North Sea (beyond is the brooding hulk of Sizewell B). However, swimmers with a sense of adventure might want to take part in their own 'sea hike' in the direction of Dunwich and enjoy a few lengths over the remains of the sunken medieval town.

Date: Weather: Your Rating: ☆ ☆ ☆ ☆ ☆

Notes:

COVEHITHE BEACH

Covehithe, Suffolk

Grid ref: TM 527818

Several miles northwards from the jolly seaside beach hut paradise of Southwold and on a stretch of coast that runs to Lowestoft, the beach at Covehithe is a different kettle of swimming fish. The sand dunes are crumbling here, and the road ends at the cliff top, the rest of it long gone into history. Down on the beach tree trunks dot the sand, reminders of the impermanence of the coast in this part of eastern England. One day the sea will claim all as it carries out its war of attrition on the land. But for now put such gloomy thoughts aside and enjoy a thoughtful swim in the brisk and stimulating waters of the North Sea. This is one for the swimmer who wants a challenge, who wants to be provoked into thinking about why they swim. There's also a rich variety of birdlife here to watch as you commune with the water.

Date: Weather: Your Rating: ☆ ☆ ☆ ☆ ☆

Notes:

3 EMBLETON BAY

Nr Embleton, Northumberland

Grid ref: NU 247225

Take a dip in the shadow of history. At the southern end of Embleton's wide, curving sandy beach the dramatic-looking castle of Dunstanburgh stands on a headland looking out to sea, one of the famous Northumbrian castles that speak of the tumultuous past of this gorgeous part of northern England. This is a marvellous spot with the North Sea ahead of you and windswept sand dunes behind, home to a group of beach chalets built in the 1930s by golfers who wanted to stay in the area. It's also a great family friendly spot – beach cricket is a must and young ones will enjoy a paddle – and when the rollers start to liven up a bit, it's popular with watersports enthusiasts, so it's best to take a swim when the waters are calmer. Hungry wild swimmers will find relief in the nearby village of Craster, where the famous kippers come from.

Date: Weather: Your Rating: ☆ ☆ ☆ ☆ ☆

Notes:

CAERFAI BAY

St David's, Pembrokeshire

Grid ref: SM 7624

This is the closest beach to the historic cathedral city of St David's and it's an idyllic spot, surrounded by high cliffs and offering seaward views out towards the islands of Skomer and Skokholm. Swimming takes place in a clear blue sea and the beach offers a gentle slope into deeper waters. There's another bonus: its south-facing situation means that after the swim you can enjoy the cove's suntrap status, surrounded by high cliffs. To get to it, you can either walk or drive down a narrow road before you come to a car park overlooking the cove. A rugged walk down the cliff path brings you to the sandy beach. When the tide is in and you fancy a bit more privacy, there's a small quiet cove to the left, which is worth swimming to, though as the tide recedes expect to be joined by more people. Seals are often seen.

Date: Weather: Your Rating: ☆ ☆ ☆ ☆ ☆

Notes:

5 HOLKHAM BEACH

Nr Wells-next-the-Sea, Norfolk

Grid ref: TF 919451

Those who saw *Shakespeare in Love* might recall Gwyneth Paltrow at the end of the movie strolling across a massive open stretch of sand beneath a wide sky. That was Holkham Beach, but why let Hollywood stars have all the fun? This is more of a landscape than just a beach and it plugs right into what we tend to think of as the substance of classic childhood holidays: endless blue sky, golden sands that seem to go on for ever and on which castles are waiting to be built and a shimmering surface of sea in the distance. For those with an interest in wildlife the bay is home to one of the UK's largest coastal reserves and for swimmers the water quality is excellent, so there's no excuse for not dashing to its edge. A couple of caveats: the current can be strong, and regulars recommend wearing surf shoes as a protection against weaverfish stings.

Date: Weather: Your Rating: ☆ ☆ ☆ ☆ ☆

Notes:

6 ACHMELVICH BEACH

Nr Lochinver, Sutherland, Highlands

Grid ref: NC 057247

Three miles out of the port of Lochinver on the west coast of Scotland, a single-track road brings swimmers to the stunning surroundings of Achmelvich Bay, where there's a well-sheltered and expansive beach of white sand. The water is bracing out here but there's no better spot for a gentle swim on a hot summer day. This is a beautiful part of northern Scotland with plenty of walks in the area and if you turn your back to the sea you can glimpse the western edge of Suilven towering over the landscape. Those interested in exploring will discover several other bays and beaches in the area, plus an intriguing castle-like building close to the beach that was built in the 1960s. A campsite sited next to the beach means it can get busy though this has its compensations: in the summer there's a café that sells fish and chips, an ideal post-swim snack.

Date: Weather: Your Rating: ☆ ☆ ☆ ☆ ☆

Notes:

ANGEL BAY

Penrhyn Bay, Llandudno, Gwynedd

Grid ref: SH 816827

The Little Orme is at one end of Llandudno Bay (the Great Orme is at the other). This popular seaside town has two beaches which offer great family fun. However on the eastern side of the Little Orme you will find the sheltered secret cove of Angel Bay (called Porth Dyniewaid on the map). It's approached via a path from a housing estate in Penrhyn Bay and past old quarry workings and abandoned machines from the days when limestone was extracted from this headland. The cove itself has a shingle beach which shelves steeply out into deep water. It is popular with locals in the know, who also come to fish off the rocks on the eastern side of the cove (there's also the possibility of diving in this spot as well). One warning though: it is recommended that you do not swim out beyond the headland due to the danger of strong currents.

Date: Weather: Your Rating: ☆ ☆ ☆ ☆ ☆

Notes:

LUSTY GLAZE BEACH

8

Newquay, Cornwall

Grid ref: SW 822625

Even though this compact and secretive cove, which is only a short walk from the party atmosphere that is Newquay, is privately owned, it's open to the public all year round and – even better – you don't have to pay a bean to enjoy it. The reward for finding it is a beautifully sandy beach surrounded by cliffs, an ideal place for a swim. However waves can be choppy and access is via steep steps – worth remembering if you have very small children or infirm members of the older generation. Plenty of other activities are based around the beach, including an adventure centre and the home of the National Lifeguard Training Centre – this means that the beach is thoroughly patrolled by lifeguards and you can swim with the utmost confidence that it will be safe. Other activities popular in the area include – naturally – surfing (boards can be hired) and coasteering.

Date: Weather: Your Rating: ☆ ☆ ☆ ☆ ☆

Notes:

9 TALISKER BAY

Nr Carbost, Isle of Skye Grid ref: NG 313302

Beach shoes are a must on the approach over the pebbly and occasionally stony beach at Talisker Bay. There are also various bits of fishing equipment and nets dotted about, as well as the usual clumps of seaborne rubbish that drift in with the tide. So far, so unpromising. However, do persevere, as this lively Hebridean beach is a real rough diamond, a wonderful spot for doing a bit of body surfing. It's also a magnificent-looking place, surrounded by cliffs, down which a 100-foot waterfall crashes. Be prepared for a vigorous and bracing dip in the water, bearing in mind the post-swim reward of a dram of the peaty Talisker single malt that is produced nearby. There are magnificent cliff walks in the area, while it's also worth waiting to catch the wonderful sunset at the end of a glorious summer's day.

Date: Weather: Your Rating: ☆ ☆ ☆ ☆ ☆

Notes:

10 BURTON BRADSTOCK

Burton Bradstock, Dorset

Grid ref: SY 482890

A couple of miles out of the town of Bridport, the small village of Burton Bradstock sits on the world-famous Jurassic Coastline, a fascinating, rugged landscape that stretches for 95 miles. This is a long, coarsely sandy beach that is overlooked by sandstone cliffs and it offers good swimming in the clean waters (though it is recommended that you keep an eye out for strong undercurrents). It's a popular spot in the summer, though there is plenty of room, while the award-winning Hive Beach Café is a classy and friendly place for a bite to eat after a spell in the water – fresh fish and seafood are a speciality. Those with an interest in fossils also make for the beach to sift through the crumbling cliffs as they reveal their ancient treasures, so this is an ideal place for a calming swim after spending the morning going through the past.

Date: Weather: Your Rating: ☆ ☆ ☆ ☆ ☆

Notes:

11 NEW BRIGHTON

New Brighton, Wallasey, Wirral Peninsula

Grid ref: SJ 306945

Prior to the 1960s, New Brighton's long sandy beach was a top-class swimming spot with all the fun of the seaside thrown in as well, but the preference for cheap holidays in the sun plus the increase of pollution in the Mersey saw its star wane in tandem with that of the resort. However, times have changed. Investment in the area has increased and New Brighton is on the up while the water is clean and inviting again. This is a very family-friendly spot, with the beach offering nearly a mile of clean flat sand and calm waters as well as views over Liverpool Bay towards the resort's city neighbour. The North Wirral Coastal Park also starts at the King's Parade in New Brighton, offering the chance to investigate some of the natural beauty and wildlife of the peninsula, as well as producing further places for swimming.

Date: Weather: Your Rating: ☆ ☆ ☆ ☆ ☆

Notes:

12 BRIGHTON BEACH

West Pier to Palace Pier, Brighton, East Sussex

Grid ref: TQ 3003

One of the more popular challenges for swimmers who descend on Brighton Beach is the 1-kilometre crawl between the derelict West Pier and the Palace Pier (the latter is very much alive with its funfair and bright and breezy atmosphere). It's a tradition that dates back to the years after the Second World War and is still popular despite the health and safety misgivings of the authorities. That said, this is definitely one for the strong swimmer as there can be a bit of drag in the water when the waves hit the sloping shingle beach. Furthermore, at high tide, the water can get deep within a couple of metres offshore – this is certainly a swim not to be attempted alone and be sure to let a lifeguard know what you are doing. These concerns notwithstanding it's an enjoyable and popular challenge – weather permitting of course!

Date: Weather: Your Rating: ☆ ☆ ☆ ☆ ☆

Notes:

13 BARRICANE BEACH

Nr Woolacombe, North Devon

Grid ref: SS 4544

North of the vast and sprawling pleasure beach of Woolacombe, where surfers and swimmers vie with each other for space in the sea, Barricane Beach is a small but equally sandy cove that offers a quieter alternative to its popular neighbour. It is also a very attractive beach for families. The water is safe for swimming, while children will love to explore (and splash in) the rock pools when the tide is out. Meanwhile those with an interest in seashells can beachcomb for all manner of exotic ones (including cowries), which will have drifted across from the Caribbean courtesy of the Gulf Stream; it's not for nothing that locals have long nicknamed it 'Shell Beach'. Be aware though that the beach is only accessible during low tide. Grunta Beach is the next cove up, small and secret, getting its name from a shipload of pigs that was wrecked there, with the beasts all coming ashore grunting!

Date: Weather: Your Rating: ☆ ☆ ☆ ☆ ☆

Notes:

KENNACK SANDS

Nr Ruan Minor, Cornwall

Grid ref: SW 7316

The beach at Kennack Sands is divided into two parts, separated by a small hill and bundle of rocks. Most folk settle down on the first beach, which is where dogs are allowed, but if you're mutt-less then it's worth walking on the path above the beach to get to the next stretch of sand (which is also a nature reserve). Here there are fewer people, even during the peak of the summer season, which means that you get to enjoy a nice quiet swim in the clear blue waters, though be aware of the undercurrents the further out you go. Some swimmers have reputedly swum with dolphins that have been drawn to the area, so if you see a fin in the water it should be Flipper rather than Jaws! Due to the fact that the beach has a large tidal range, it is also popular with surfers. There is a lifeguard post on the first beach.

Date: Weather: Your Rating: ☆ ☆ ☆ ☆ ☆

Notes:

15 BURGH ISLAND

Bigbury on Sea, Devon

Grid ref: SX 650441

When the tide is out there's a golden stretch of sand exposed between the Devon mainland and Burgh Island, whose art deco hotel was so beloved of Agatha Christie that she located one of her whodunits there. Swimmers with adventure in mind have been known to enjoy a watery perambulation around the island, and those who have participated suggest setting off in an anti-clockwise direction when the high tide has slackened (with the tide in, you need to cross over by the famous 'sea tractor'). It's an inspiring swim with the high cliffs of the island above, the odd sighting of a seal and occasionally you might even come face to face with a spearfisherman in search of sea bass or mullet. Afterwards, as the tide goes out, you can enjoy a spot of body boarding and skimming on the exposed beach before heading to the Pilchard Inn for a refreshing pint.

Date: Weather: Your Rating: ☆ ☆ ☆ ☆ ☆

Notes:

POOLS, PONDS AND MERES

Around the country there is a plethora of naturally formed ponds, pools and meres, still and calm places that work their magic well on the wild swimmer. Some are high up on peaty moorland, while others have a more natural origin and were formed during the age of the glaciers. Many are secret places, known to local people, with some of them once upon a time having a diving board attached or even a small jetty off which swimmers could leap (or dive if the water was deep enough). For the bravest and hardiest swimmers the lack of clarity in a reed-fringed mere gives an added excitement — you might be keeping company with an old eel waiting for the call to its final journey to the Sargasso Sea or, as is supposed to be in one pond high up in moorland in Staffordshire, there's the legend of a mermaid that may add spice to your swim.

FAERIE POOLS

Glen Brittle, Skye

Grid ref: NG 436257

Magic seems to hover in the air on the first encounter with the Faerie Pools of Glen Brittle. With the magnificent Black Cullin Mountains rising directly to the east, it's not that difficult to imagine that mysterious beings might have been responsible for these ice-blue, crystal-clear pools, which are part of a stream of waterfalls that flow down the slopes (despite the appearance of Mediterranean clarity and warmth their transit from the tops makes them teeth-chatteringly cold). Those in the know make for Allt Coir a Mhadaidh and enjoy a swim between a couple of pools that are connected by means of an underwater arch. The swim demands a trek, so pack walking boots, while the coldness of the water also necessitates wet suit and swimming cap, but the effort is well worth it. A similarly set of beguiling pools in the area can be found at Allt a' Choire Ghreadaich (NG 417230).

Date: Weather: Your Rating: ☆ ☆ ☆ ☆ ☆

Notes:

LINHOPE SPOUT

Breamish River, near Ingram, Northumberland

Grid ref: NT 959171

Northumberland is God's own walking country, a place of isolated moorland, deep valleys, craggy outcrops and spectacular sights such as the Linhope Spout, a 60-foot water chute near the village of Linhope on the edge of the Cheviot Hills. This is a popular spot to cool off after a long arduous day in the hills, as it features a splendid and seemingly bottomless plunge pool underneath the spout. Adventurous older children and adults jump into the pool from a 2-metre ledge, though those daring souls with a head for heights can climb higher up for an even more exciting leap (not without checking the depth of water where they will land and making sure that there are no obstacles). For a quieter time in the water, others make for the shallows to enjoy a splash and a dip before retiring to the riverbank for a well-deserved picnic.

Date: Weather: Your Rating: ☆ ☆ ☆ ☆ ☆

Notes:

3 HAMPSTEAD PONDS

Hampstead, London

Grid ref: TQ 273862

Wild swimming in London? The Thames might not be recommended due to currents and boat traffic, but there's always the Serpentine Lido. However, for something that's a bit wilder and closer to nature then the famous Hampstead Ponds high up on the Heath are just the job. They were dug as reservoirs several centuries ago and were fed (and still are) by the River Fleet, but they began to be used for swimming, starting with the men's pool, at the end of the nineteenth century. Fans of swimming out here claim that the Kenwood Ladies' Pond is the best-looking one, as it lies in the shade of oak trees, which are especially attractive in leaf. Funnily enough, the Men's Bath Pool is the biggest of the three. Both the single-sex pools have their ardent fans, though some newcomers might find them a mite cliquey. The Mixed Pool is more relaxed and offers a grassy area for sunbathing.

Date: Weather: Your Rating: ☆ ☆ ☆ ☆ ☆

Notes:

4 ST NECTAN'S KIEVE

Near Tintagel, Cornwall

Grid ref: SX 081885

This is King Arthur country. Close to Tintagel, with its impressive clifftop castle that may or may not have been Camelot, St Nectan's Kieve (the latter word is Cornish for pool) is a secluded gorge in which a 60-foot double waterfall gushes into a decent-sized plunge pool (it passes through a sizeable arch in the rocks on its descent which makes it even more stunning). These are holy waters: Arthur and his knights were supposed to have been baptised here. Meanwhile, further spiritual resonance is given to the Kieve by the renowned Cornish holy man St Nectan, who allegedly made himself at home here in the sixth century. This gives the place a symbolic value for many, who believe it to be sacred, so for that reason wild swimmers are asked to take their dip with respect. There is an entrance fee of £3.

Date: Weather: Your Rating: ☆ ☆ ☆ ☆ ☆

Notes:

5 BELSTONE

River Taw, Belstone, Dartmoor, Devon

Grid ref: SX 621930

It goes without saying that one of the cardinal rules of wild swimming is to watch where the locals go – they represent generations of knowledge about the best places for a splash. One such place, where locals have swum for years, is a pool on the River Taw as it comes off Dartmoor before circumventing the moorland village of Belstone and heading for its meeting with the Bristol Channel, 45 miles to the north. Follow the Taw up from Belstone, in the direction of Belstone Tor, and after 30 minutes of walking you will come to a deep pool that offers a cool and refreshing dip. This is a narrow and deep swimming hole that remains fairly cold and bracing throughout the year, so you might prefer to seek it out on a hot summer's day. The water is brown, but that's only the result of the peat on the moor.

Date: Weather: Your Rating: ☆ ☆ ☆ ☆ ☆

Notes:

FRENSHAM GREAT POND

6

Frensham, Surrey

Grid ref: SU 846405

Back in the Middle Ages the Bishop of Winchester had this pond dug to hold a stock of carp that would supply his dinner table. Nowadays the church's ownership has been replaced by that of the National Trust who run it in conjunction with the local council and make a very good job of it. Sunny days see it eminently popular with families who flock to its wide sandy beach – small children build castles and then paddle in the shallows while their more daring older siblings and parents enjoy a dip in the separate, 50-metre wide designated swimming area (the pond also allows sailing and fishing). There is a lifeguard in the summer. The neighbouring Little Pond is a haven for wildlife and no swimming is allowed there. Relatively easy access, a gently sloping sandy beach, warm water and a small café – what more could the laid-back wild swimmer want?

Date: Weather: Your Rating: ☆ ☆ ☆ ☆ ☆

Notes:

7 STAINFORTH FORCE

Stainforth, Settle, North Yorkshire

Grid ref: SD 818671

Yorkshire folk and Lancastrians might pretend to be mortal enemies but the River Ribble at least unites them, passing at it does through the two neighbouring counties. On the Yorkshire stretch, close to the village of Stainforth with the river still meandering down from the Dales, swimmers from near and far come for the trio of popular pools: Fosse, Long Eel and Robin Hood. All are deep enough for a spot of jumping, with Long Eel recommended as the one in which a decent swim can be undertaken. There are also some shallower ones suitable for younger children. A further benefit is the limestone ledge over which the river plummets just after passing beneath an old stone bridge, offering the chance of a refreshing shower. Afterwards, if it's a hot sunny day, there are flat grown-up stones on which you can lie and soak up the sun before enjoying a picnic.

Date: Weather: Your Rating: ☆ ☆ ☆ ☆ ☆

Notes:

MERMAID'S POOL

8

Thorncliffe, nr Leek, Staffordshire Grid ref: SK 040613

Waters and rivers were venerated by ancient peoples, who populated them with gods and demons and all manner of water spirits. The folk who lived around here in the shadow of the craggy outcrops of the Roaches had a different idea and, as the name might suggest, a mermaid lays claim to this peat-stained pool high up on moorland north of Leek. It is not any old mermaid either – this scaly lady had a bad reputation and would create mayhem for anyone unwise enough to take a dip in her abode. Modern wild swimmers are made of sterner stuff and will want to splash about in the murky but fresh waters of the pool (also called Blakesmere) just to say that they have swum with a mermaid! Look for the pool on the moorland close to the Mermaid Inn, which is off the A53. Not suitable for children because of its steep sides.

Date: Weather: Your Rating: ☆ ☆ ☆ ☆ ☆

Notes:

9 GOLITHA FALLS

Near St Cleer, Cornwall

Grid ref: SX 223687

The River Fowey rises up on Bodmin Moor and, although it's still in its infancy when it travels through the area named Golitha Falls, there's a sense of urgency and excitement as it tumbles through a shadowed green world of ancient woodland. This is a beautiful stretch of countryside, part of a Natural England nature reserve, and you will come across remnants of the old copper mine that once operated out here. There are opportunities for paddling in the shallows, but there's also a plunge pool that can be reached by walking downstream along the main path. When this comes to an end, continue along the rocks (take care as many are mossy) for a few more minutes before reaching the hidden and secretive pool. On a hot summer's day this offers a heavenly chance of a quiet dip, but it is recommended that you swim against the current.

Date: Weather: Your Rating: ☆ ☆ ☆ ☆ ☆

Notes:

LYN POOL

10 Rockford, nr Lynton, Devon

Grid ref: SS 754488

Rockford is a very small but handsomely located hamlet to be found in Exmoor's Doone country, in a deep wooded valley where the red deer roam and buzzards wheel in the sky above. The East Lyn passes through the valley and if you cross to the northern side of the river over the footbridge opposite the Rockford Inn, then a 10-minute stroll downriver along the bank will bring you to Lyn Pool (in fact there are a series of pools in the area). This is crystal-clear water but it is cold even at the height of the summer (locals recommend a wet suit) as not much sunlight gets through the canopy of trees. The pool is deep enough for a plunge, while younger swimmers enjoy body-boarding into the water. The river is also popular with salmon fishermen but just use your common sense and all will be happy.

Date: Weather: Your Rating: ☆ ☆ ☆ ☆ ☆

Notes:

11 EASDALE ISLAND

Easdale Island, Oban, Argyll

Grid ref: SX 621930

Easdale Island can be found 16 miles south of Oban and was once part of the 'Islands of Slate', a group of islands in this part of the Inner Hebrides whose products were sent all over the British Empire. The industry is dead now, and one consequence of Easdale's past industrial heritage is that it is dotted with several water-filled quarries. One of these, an L-shaped one sited next to the sea on the western edge of the island, has become a popular swimmers' pool and its appeal is easy to understand – clear blue water that is a direct invitation to dive right in. It also has a little beach. Another aspect of the island's charm is that it is completely car-free – it's a short ferry-ride from the mainland or you might want to swim it as some do every year. After a swim do take time to wander about the island and appreciate getting away from it all.

Date: Weather: Your Rating: ☆ ☆ ☆ ☆ ☆

Notes:

12 KISDON FORCE

Keld, North Yorkshire

Grid ref: NY 898010

Canoeists and wild swimmers seeking a challenge can do no better than visit Kisdon Force, a wooded gorge that features a brace of exuberant waterfalls as the River Swale bubbles and foams its way down from the North Yorkshire Dales. Canoeists see their way to navigate the falls which, although not dangerously steep, still offer a lure for thrill-seekers, while swimmers find solace in two plunge pools. The highest pool is the largest and offers ledges from which to jump, while down below the second pool is deeper with steeper walls and a bit more in shade – not one for novices. The Force can be found close to the town of Keld and there are camping facilities in the area if you want to explore further. Obviously, if there has been heavy rain be aware of the Swale, as it has been noted for its unpredictability in the past.

Date: Weather: Your Rating: ☆ ☆ ☆ ☆ ☆

Notes:

13 PWLLAU MAEN MAWR

Glyntawe, Powys

SN 853257.

This is yet another swimming spot that has been nurtured and enjoyed by generations of locals since before the swimming pool wove its chlorinated charms, so if you're in the area then why not join them for a dip? It's especially suitable if you have children with you. Pwll means pool in Welsh and there are a group of paddling pools (pwllau is the plural) standing on the River Tawe as it comes down from the Black Mountain. This is very safe section of the river and the kids will have a great time splashing about and running in and out of the water. Finding the pools is not that difficult either: head north out of Glyntawe and then hang a left by the pub. A couple of miles on, the Maen Mawr standing stones (including a stone circle) are on your left and it's time to get in the water.

Date: Weather: Your Rating: ☆ ☆ ☆ ☆ ☆

Notes:

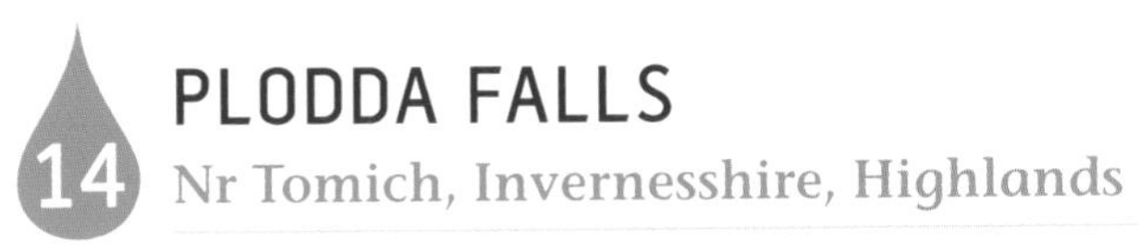

14 PLODDA FALLS

Nr Tomich, Invernesshire, Highlands

Grid ref: NH 277238

There's nothing better for an outdoor swimmer than to splash about in the midst of some spectacular scenery; it adds lustre to the experience. A case in point is Plodda Falls, which has more than its fair share of natural beauty, set as it is in the midst of a stunning forest of Douglas Fir and European Larch. At 46 metres it's also Scotland's highest waterfall, a cascade of ice-cold water rushing to meet its destiny in a deep plunge pool that offers invigorating opportunities for both diving and swimming. A good level of fitness is a necessity in order to reach this tremendous spot though, as it involves a steady hike of at least half-an-hour through the forest plus a scramble that some might find challenging. The reward for this adventurous trek, however, is immense as you swim within earshot of thundering, crystal-clear Highland water.

Date: Weather: Your Rating: ☆ ☆ ☆ ☆ ☆

Notes:

SWIMMING TIPS

Swimming is good for you, helping to tone your body and improve cardiovascular performance; outdoor swimming is even better as it combines health benefits with the joy of being at one with nature. If you can swim then wild swimming is for you. However, swimming outdoors is different from going up and down a heated and safe indoor pool – you are at the mercy of the weather, turbulence on the water's surface caused by wind and you need to know where you are going. Unless you're a keen swimmer, a member of a club, or someone who has lived the life aquatic since being a babe in arms, then there is always room to improve your technique. Recent research has indicated that out of the 12 million Britons who swim, the majority have a poor swimming performance which means that they are not reaping the full benefits of being in the water. Here are five ways in which your swimming can be improved.

- If using the front crawl, exhale when the head is submerged. Learn to breathe on both sides when the head surfaces.
- Learn to keep your legs, arms and head working together in harmony.
- Keep the body horizontal from head to toe as this helps to maintain a streamlined movement and cuts down on drag.
- Sustain an even leg kick — legs only provide a small part of propulsion but they do help to keep the body level.
- If using breaststroke try to move smoothly as you complete every stroke.

WILD SWIMMING SAFETY

Like any other outside activity such as climbing or surfing, there are certain aspects of safety to be considered with wild swimming. These are basic common sense rather than the kind of health and safety that would have us all wrapped up in cotton wool. Here are five points to think on when you have the urge to wild swim.

- One of the most obvious caveats, which is something that should be drilled into every swimmer, wild or otherwise, is never go into the water under the influence of alcohol.
- If you can, try and swim with someone else for company. It's not only more fun but if you get into difficulty then you have someone to help you out.
- If you're keen on diving into water then always make sure you know the depth. Some tidal outdoor pools will have sand in them that shifts with every tide, while some rivers might have underwater obstacles. If you're new to a stretch of water ask the locals. Always be aware of the time of tides where potentially difficult currents can be found.
- Getting tangled up in riverweed can cause a bit of a scare so avoid when necessary, while some rivers also have blue-green algae, which should be avoided as it can cause sickness. Urban rivers and canals can be risky due to the possibility of rat-borne Weil's disease. Cover cuts with waterproof plasters.
- Exceptionally cold water can be a drain on body heat, so it might be worth looking at a wetsuit if you are going to be in cold water for anything more than a reviving Boxing Day dip.

WATER TEMPERATURE

'Come on in, the water's lovely' might be a phrase heard a lot on a Mediterranean beach, but it's not so commonplace in Britain where both fresh and salt water take time to warm up during the summer. Generally speaking, if you've been used to heated indoor pools, outdoor swimming will come as a bit of a shock – the water can be cold but it also will be bracing and get your pulse racing. Witness the crowd of swimmers who take an icy plunge on Boxing Day, no doubt to purge the body after the excesses of the previous day.

The best way to enter the water is a case of personal choice; some people dash in, while others wade in slowly. It is a matter of getting acclimatised without hypothermia setting in. Expert wild swimmers recommend that a water temperature of 15°C is best for novices. For spells in the water longer than a brief splash a wetsuit can be useful; it also helps with buoyancy. In more inclement weather, for instance a swim in the autumn, especially in a mountain lake, a wetsuit becomes a must (some suggest triathlon wetsuits that are especially suited for swimming rather than the sort surfers wear). If the water is too cold and you find your teeth chattering and a headache developing, then come out, quickly don warm and dry clothes and engage in some physical activity to warm yourself up. Know your limits – if the water is cold don't start on a marathon swim that might see you losing energy some way from the shore. Other useful equipment includes goggles, swimming hat, beach or river shoes and wetsuit boots and gloves.

WATERLOG

Roger Deakin's *Waterlog* is the bible of wild swimming, being an endearingly eccentric and elegiac account of the author's attempts to swim across a variety of waters in the UK at the end of the 1990s. It was an idea partially influenced by John Cheever's melancholy short story *The Swimmer* (made into a film starring Burt Lancaster as the man who tries to swim home across the pools of suburbia) with further inspiration occurring as he drifted through the soft waters of the moat that surrounded his home in Suffolk.

Thus began a journey that would see Deakin try the patience of fly-fishermen on the Test, seek out the fresh and zesty springs and outdoor pools of the Malverns, stick two fingers up to the law by diving into the massive drains that cross the Fens and rhapsodise as he came across lidos of varying age and condition. In carrying out his water-borne odyssey Deakin came up with a wonder of nature writing that managed to fuse his meditations on wild swimming with canny and careful observations of nature – both human and wild. It is beautifully written with a warm and human voice that alternates between philosophical reflections on swimming and an unabashed celebration of the waterways and pools that criss-cross the country (he was a founder member of Friends of the Earth so the environment was never far from his thoughts). Sadly, Deakin died in 2006, but left behind a book that would inspire wild swimmers of all abilities and ages.

WATERWORKS

Even though wild swimmers like to spend as much of their time in the water as they can manage, there is a growing number of books that should tempt them to reach for the towel and curl up in the corner.

The essential must-have is the late Roger Deakin's seminal *Waterlog* (Vintage), a warm and wonderful account of the author's journey around the rivers, lakes, lidos and even waterways of the UK – it's a travelogue, nature notes, philosophical thoughts, history, culture and swimming guide all wrapped in one book. In a similarly thoughtful view, Charles Sprawson's *Haunts of the Black Masseur* (Vintage), celebrates the swimmer as a cultural icon, whether it's Byron making a splash in the Hellespont or Johnny Weissmuller in his Tarzan loincloth.

Daniel Start's brace of books *Wild Swimming* and *Wild Swimming Coast* (Punk Publishing) are lively guidebooks to Britain's rivers, lakes and hidden coastal spots. Kate Rew's *Wild Swim* (Guardian Books) is a handsome-looking coffee-table style book with over three hundred outdoor swims – from lido to lake to idyllic country river.

If it is history you're after then Janet Smith's *Liquid Assets* (English Heritage/Malavan Media) is a thorough history of British lidos. It is a book that takes a look at the lido's role in British social life, from their beginnings in the nineteenth century through to the golden age of lidos in the 1930s. There are plenty of nostalgic photographs and a unique list of all the lidos still open and pleasing the crowds.